In Your Twenties, How to be Better with Money

Authored by:
W.R. Marsons

In collaboration with:
Investments Working Group

First Edition – January 2023

About the Author

W.R. Marsons is an entrepreneur with businesses in the IT services industry based out of Austin, Texas, United States and London, United Kingdom.

He has multiple years of diverse business experience built on a hands-on approach through trial and error. He has built his most recent one after learning from multiple failures in his early years, managing debt, and understanding how business and money operate in the markets today.

He has engineered the development of businesses in the Imports, Travel and Tourism, Food and Beverage, IT Services, Education Consultancy, and Industrial Manufacturing. over the past seven years.

He has a Bachelors degree in Mechanical Engineering and a Masters Degree in Accounting in Finance from two of the UK's most prestigious institutes.

About Investments Working Group

<u>Investments Working Group</u> offers a range of services and support to help people navigate their lives and be more careful and prudent with their finances. We offer services and resources such as:

Financial Education & Non-advisory Help
Learn Budgeting, Money Management, and Planning
Free Helpful Resources on the website.
Non-advisory Product Recommendations

Our authors have years of expertise in educating people about their finances and helping them make smarter financial decisions. They aim to guide clients through their current money needs and set long-term goals to achieve financial independence.

Contents

Introduction...6

   Good Debt vs. Bad Debt.......................................8

   The Importance of a Good Credit Score................9

Chapter 1 Define Your Financial Goals................11

   Avoiding a Debt Trap...12

   Setting Financial Goals.......................................13

   Short-term Financial Goals..................................16

   Mid-term Financial Goals.....................................19

   Long-term Financial Goals...................................22

   Goals and Financial Independence......................24

Chapter 2 Bad Money Habits You Need to Let Go.....25

   Bad Habits to Bad Debts......................................26

   Bad Debts and Increased Liability........................27

   Common Bad Money Habits.................................28

   Re-evaluating Financial Habits for Improvement.....37

Chapter 3 Good Money Habits You Need to Take Up.....38

   Good Habits to Good Debt....................................41

   Good Money Habits..42

   Being Responsible and Establishing Good Habits.....51

Chapter 4 Creating a Budget Using the 50-30-20 Model.....52

   Why Budget?..54

   The 50-30-20 Budgeting Model............................56

   Create your 50-30-20 Budget...............................60

Accurate Calculation, Disciplined Spending 62

Chapter 5 How to Live a Life of Financial Freedom 63

Taking Advantage of your 20s 64

Looking into the Future 67

Diversifying Portfolio to Maximize Returns 73

Conclusion..75

Managing Money, Saving, and Investing......................................76

Preparing Now, Indulging Later 77

You're not Alone in your Financial Journey 77

Introduction

Getting lost in a financial struggle when first entering the job market is easy. As we move into full-time work, saving money might become a secondary goal. There is, after all, always something to spend it on. But the fact is that saving right now might not seem important, now is when it's crucial.

Saving money does not only refer to retirement savings. Although that is important, it isn't the only factor to consider. As someone just entering full-time work, we may have an optimistic outlook on our financial future. That's a good attitude, but it can leave us unprepared.

The truth is that circumstances can change. While we hope we never stray into difficult times, it's best to be prepared for them. That's not the only reason to start saving up in your early working years. Saving now will make a lot of things easier down the road. A young artist shares how she learned the importance of saving:

"When I was younger and first started earning, I saw my income as a way to buy fancy shoes and clothes. When my friends started planning a last-minute trip to Japan, I realized my budget did not allow for spontaneity. I began saving to be able to follow bigger dreams. Soon after, I lost my job and found out I needed surgery. Without health insurance, I would have been broke and on the streets. Today I run my own business, earning a good income and doing what I love because I was able to keep myself afloat during the most difficult period of my life by thinking ahead."

In addition to preparing for potential emergencies, savings are a financial cushion for the future. Our lifestyles get more expensive as we age, and not saving until later in life can make living comfortably more difficult. It is a greater burden, and you will constantly feel like you're falling short. However, you can achieve financial independence even with some good debt.

Good Debt vs. Bad Debt

As of 2020, the average American in their 20s and 30s has over $10,000 to $20,000 in non-mortgage debt. Add homeowners to that and you have debts over $200,000. But is that debt bad, or does it hinder financial independence? Not necessarily.

Good Debt

Debt that improves your quality of life in significant ways is good. One of the most common examples of this is student loans. There are about 45 million borrowers who have taken out student loans as of 2022. These loans have gone towards improving earning potential and employability.

Similarly, debts to invest in real estate or a start-up have good value. If you're just starting and hoping to build up your own business, the majority of your investment will likely be procured through a loan. This is good debt because it adds value and increases the ability to repay the loan once the business takes off.

Bad Debts

Similarly, bad debts leave you indebted without adding value to your potential. They fund purchases that neither supplement income nor add value. This seriously hurts your credit score and ability to get approved for future loans or higher credit limits. A fresh graduate from Maryland shares the harrowing story of trying to overcome credit card debt:

"After I lost my job, I began to dip into my savings. Eventually, they ran out while I struggled to find employment. I began using my credit card to make ends meet without even realizing how far into debt I was going. I began to default on my credit cards, and the amount I owed just kept building up. Now, seven years later, I have a stable income, but I am still paying off my cards, and my credit is ruined."

The Importance of a Good Credit Score

Maintaining a good credit score is an essential factor in achieving financial independence. We all think a little bit of debt is okay, and it can be, depending on the type. However, your financial planning should start with your credit score. Generally, a score between 740-799 is considered excellent, but those in lower ranges can cause difficulty. Here are some of the reasons it's important:

Improved chances of loan approval

A good credit score speaks to a person's spending habits. It shows lenders you are financially responsible and repay outstanding debts on time. This increases lender confidence and gives you a better chance of being approved for a credit card or loan.

Higher limits

Not only are lenders more willing to lend to someone with a good credit score, but they are also more likely to approve a higher borrowing limit. The amount you can borrow on a poor score is seriously limited, and lenders may levy other conditions for their security.

Better interest and insurance rates

Good credit scores almost always lead to lower interest rates on loans. The lower cost of borrowing leaves you in the position to pay off the debt faster. Your credit score also plays into insurance calculations, as there is a greater risk attached to borrowers with a low score. Good credit scores can win you low insurance premiums.

Chapter 1

Define Your Financial Goals

Financial planning becomes an essential process once you move into the workforce. Planning for the future in your 20s may seem unimportant at the time; many of us think we will have time to plan and save later on. However, our financial decisions in our 20s will affect our lives and financial position for many years.

Considering the current financial situation in the country, it is imperative to start thinking about saving. With many struggling to keep up with their needs amidst inflation and unemployment, money management can cushion future hardships. You can cultivate financial security in the early years by creating discipline and understanding how to prevent debts and save money.

Avoiding a Debt Trap

One of the worst consequences of poor financial planning I have seen is a debt trap. The financially draining cycle of increased borrowing to pay off previous debts will often spiral out of control. Hence, the amount you owe keeps mounting without hope of repayment. A financial advisor from Chicago explains how a debt trap is created:

"Let's assume the income you are earning is simply insufficient to pay off a debt- your options are to pay it off as soon as possible or let the interest rate on your outstanding loan pile up. Eventually, you might find yourself taking out new loans to clear the piled-up interest. That's a debt trap."

In addition to creating a significant financial burden that severely impacts your life, it can also lead to psychological stress. Debt traps can become hard to escape, and many people find total recovery near impossible.

Setting Financial Goals

Given the current state of the economy and the struggles we are facing today, you ought to begin planning your finances as early as possible. Because many of us wrongly believe that financial planning and money management are concerns for later in life, we cannot use the opportunities available earlier.

Creating an effective action plan also helps you think ahead for the future. Nothing needs to be set in concrete, and circumstances can always change. However, having a direction helps you work towards actual targets practically.

Why is it important to set financial goals?

When your goals are unclear, your strategies will lack direction or motivation. This is a common financial pothole people in their 20s face. Thus, it becomes hard to measure progress. There's no way to know how far you've come if you don't know where you're going. Creating accountability for yourself with your goals prevents rash decisions and keeps you on track.

Setting your financial priorities helps you keep them front and center when making decisions. This decreases the likelihood of getting off-track or making poor judgments. Especially in a crisis, we tend to think irrationally and in haste. Making contingencies and securing a financial plan for potential emergencies prevent such events from causing too much damage.

You've decided it is important to start planning your financial future. You have a vague idea of your goals and have figured out some strategies to achieve those goals. You may even have outlined a few goals for yourself. But how can you make sure that your plan is effective and purposeful?

The major component of any plan is that it needs to be goal oriented. It should focus and be built around specific financial goals you have set yourself. These can be anything, from paying off debts to saving up for a purchase, but any steps taken should pursue this goal. The best way of going about creating a goal-focused, realizable plan is by following the SMART ideology:

- **Specific:** State prominently and clearly to avoid misinterpretation, for example, "I want to buy a house."

- **Measurable:** Compute quantifiably to track progress. For example, "I should have saved up $15,000 at the end of six months."

- **Action-related:** Outline specific actions in pursuit of the goal that lead to measurable results, for example, "I will save $2,500 every month."

- **Realistic:** Do not exceed your actual capacity to fulfill them or increase your financial burden in their pursuit.

For example, if you can't save $2,500, the goal is unrealistic.

- **Time-sensitive:** Achieve goals within a realistic and doable time limit, to keep on track and monitor progress, for example, "I should have saved up for the deposit in 3 years."

SMART goals give your plan the direction to help you stay on track. With something like managing your finances, you need to stay organized with respect to your aims.

How can you adapt to your financial goals?

While being thorough with your financial goals is recommended, it does not mean they should be set in stone. No matter how well you plan, some things happen that you are not entirely prepared for. The COVID-19 pandemic is a classic case of an unexpected circumstance. Its widespread functional consequences and economic uncertainty left many vulnerable.

Any financial plan you make needs to be sensitive enough to a changing climate that it can respond immediately. It should have flexible features you can mold as the situation requires. Plan your finances, so unforeseen events do not push you too far off track.

As with changing climates, your situation may change. Initially, you plan from a starting position, but as you progress closer to your goal, it should undergo regular review. Periodically going back to the plan is also an excellent reminder of the goal and how far you have come in its pursuit.

Cash flow modeling is a useful technique I always recommend staying on track. Modeling your future income and expenses in accordance with these plans helps you predict the financial implications of any action you take in pursuit of your goals. Knowing what to expect with each decision is essential to a plan like this.

Short-term Financial Goals

Splitting goals based on the timeframe you ideally want to achieve makes the process much simpler. Short-term goals are those you wish to accomplish within the next 1-3 years. These short-term aspirations differ for everyone, but they are based mainly on your current financial situation and needs. Some common short-term financial goals include:

Budgeting for immediate needs

Establishing a budget is one of the most effective ways to ensure your money is well managed. Budgets keep your spending habits in line and prevent you from getting into bad spending habits. Start with your necessities, such as monthly grocery expenses, utilities and bills, and insurance payments.

Estimate your future expense based on your past spending on these things. Compare that in light of your income, and ensure your necessities are met without burdening you. When it comes to more infrequent or luxury expenses, your best option would be to include in your budgeting an amount to save up each month, to reach that spending goal.

A significant financial blunder is relying entirely on your earning potential and blowing everything you have on a single vacation. Ultimately, you dig a major financial hole that can be hard to recover from. Budgeting and saving are an especially great option in the face of the alternative, which is often using a credit card to meet expenses. That may afford you the vacation but also drive you deeper into debt.

Additionally, saving for emergencies is always recommended as a SMART financial goal. Such savings should cover 3 to 6 months of living expenses. The idea behind this is that, in case there are any future unforeseen emergencies, there is always a financial cushion to rely on.

Paying off credit cards

As we discussed earlier, credit card debt can be crippling and hard to get out of. You should address this as quickly as possible to avoid interest piling up on your debt. The additional benefit is that paying off your card in full before your 0% APR period expires is that you will not incur any interest.

APR free period

This Annualized Percentage Rate (APR) is the interest charged monthly and added to your credit card statement with every debt. The APR-free period, usually six to 21 months, is interest-free, and short-term goals can focus on paying off the card before the period is up.

Debt snowball

One pay-off strategy is the **debt snowball** method. This involves paying off the smallest of your debts first, progressing to the larger ones slowly. By attacking your smallest debt and making minimum payments on the rest, you gain momentum and gradually pay off all credit cards in full.

Debt avalanche

Alternatively, the **debt avalanche** method involves paying the minimum on all your debts, except the one with the highest interest rate. The extra money goes towards the credit card with the highest interest rate so that you can pay it off quicker.

Debt settlement

While **debt settlement** is also a technique available to you, whereby you settle the debt with a lump sum for less than what you owe, it can hurt your credit score. The credit report reflects that your account was settled for less, as you could not pay it off in full.

Mid-term Financial Goals

Medium-term financial goals are defined by the time period in which they are to be achieved. Typically, the target is to fulfill these goals in between 3 to 5 years. Many people are confused as to where these goals lie. A financial planning advisor explains in these simple terms:

"Mid-term goals are the bridge between short- and long-term goals, which tie those two together. These goals rely on fulfilled short-term targets to enable you to set and realistically achieve your long-term goals."

Once you've taken care of the immediate debt with your short-term goals, mid-term goals give you better cash flow to plan for future savings. Some of the things people in their 20s should focus on at this stage are:

Life and disability income insurance

Life insurance is not only a protective cushion but also a crucial facet of financial planning. It is directly related to planning better and achieving other goals. One of your options here is to get **term life insurance**, which is temporary financial protection. It can range between five to 30 years and operates at a fixed, low cost.

Term life insurance is best suited for fulfilling mid-term goals, for example, funding a child's education or care costs. This time of insurance is especially suited to those adults with significant, temporary financial needs, as they get more coverage at a lower price.

Disability income (DI) insurance protects you financially should you sustain a debilitating injury that prevents you from working. The income is provided through short-term and long-term coverage but only covers about 45%-65% of your gross income. This safeguard prevents you from falling into a financial rut due to an accident.

It is important to note that insurance applications will require medical underwriting. This is a medical evaluation for private insurance to determine premiums, benefit limits, and even if you qualify. This will also determine which health conditions the policy covers. The underwriting generally includes:

- Previous and current medical history
- Height and weight
- Family medical history
- Occupation

Student loans

Student loan debt can be the central focus of mid-term financial goals. Once short-term goals are met and debts settled, student loans should be one of the medium-term focuses. Paying them as early as possible has a lot of advantages. It is a much better option than including these loans in your debt payment plan for a multitude of reasons. For example, it will:

- Make focusing on and achieving other financial goals easier by reducing your debt-to-income ratio. This also improves the chances of being approved for a mortgage.

- Decrease the cost of loans and interest payments. The tax break is limited in efficacy and does not provide substantial financial motivation to delay paying off your loans.

- Reduce the financial stress associated with being able to make payments, also freeing up your finances for other investments.

Deferment and forbearance

Many people may choose to deal with student loans by deferment or forbearance. A **deferment** lets you stop making payments on your loans for up to 3 years. This, however, is not loan forgiveness, and you will still owe the full amount plus accrued interest at the end of the period. You should only use this method if you expect to be able to pay a lump sum later on.

A deferral won't directly impact your credit score, but it increases the age and size of the loan. That can hurt your score. Additionally, the deferment period will be excluded from consideration if you are ever looking for loan forgiveness. You will need to resume payment to be considered.

Student loan **forbearance** lets you stop or reduce payments for up to 12 months. However, interest will continue to gather for the period of non-payment. The result will be that capitalization will cause more interest to accrue over time. Any repayment plans will see increased monthly payments from that point forth.

Make room in your plans for things you have always wanted to do, such as traveling or learning a new skill. This kind of planning will ensure you can realize your dreams and stay on track for a stable and fulfilling future.

Long-term Financial Goals

Your short- and mid-term financial goals prepare you for long-term goals, which is where your financial plan culminates. These goals should picture what your life should look like overall, and you need to set other targets so that they result in the fulfillment of long-term financial goals. Financial planning is all about preparing for events that are still far away.

Retirement plan

A significant focus of long-term goals is to plan for your retirement. While it may appear very far off in your 20s, making a retirement plan early helps you prepare for exactly what you want.

The first step to creating a retirement plan with supporting financial goals is identifying your retirement needs.

I always encourage my clients to develop some idea of what they would expect at that time. You should consider estimated expenses at such a time and what your source and amount of income might be. Things like rent or mortgage payments should take into consideration. Your current savings plans should have long-term features to meet estimated future needs.

The most common options include a 401(k) or an individual retirement account (IRA). A 401(k) is an employer-sponsored retirement fund, where tax breaks are offered on the amount invested from the employee's paycheck into the fund. An IRA is sponsored by the individual themselves with a financial institution and allows tax breaks on contributions.

Participating in company retirement programs can be more beneficial as they can consist of an additional company contribution. The general rule is to put away 15% of your pre-tax income for retirement.

You should also look into automated savings and limiting spending as potential ways to increase retirement savings. Automating the process will ensure you are saving up, no matter what. Other options can also become available to you past a certain age, such as catch-up contributions to increase your retirement fund. These let you save up more than the annual limits allow, to make up for the time you weren't saving during earlier years.

House down payment

An additional focus may be on owning property. While most people set this goal, the current economy has made buying or owning a home difficult. Many young people are now forced to rent or move back in with their parents. This has made it even more vital for you to focus savings on a long-term investment like that.

You will also be able to build your equity in an appreciating asset. Again, this future planning will require knowing what kind of home you want to buy and saving accordingly. Contacting experts in this field would also be suitable to help you figure out how to plan far into the future.

Goals and Financial Independence

At the end of the day, your financial plan should produce an interconnected image of your goals. Your short-term goals should lead to medium-term goals, which should further lead to long-term goals. While setting responsible targets that sustainably improve your quality of life is essential, they shouldn't be your only focus.

Chapter 2

Bad Money Habits You Need to Let Go

Moving into the workforce and starting your career can be exciting. You are ready to learn new skills, apply your knowledge and skills to your job, and look forward to climbing the ladder to success. Another upside is finally earning enough to make your own financial decisions. With that also comes a disturbing trend in the spending habits of people in their 20s.

Bad Habits to Bad Debts

In 2022, credit card debt for Americans surpassed $887 billion, a $46 billion increase from the first quarter. Bad money habits in your early years make for a poor financial future. Unfortunately, people in their 20s often fall into this trap.

They can start with indulging in immediate gratification: buying and spending on things that fulfill an immediate purpose but add no value to your life or financial standing for the future. These habits also include indulging in non-essentials to the point of having nothing left over from your paycheck every month.

Constantly engaging in habits, you cannot afford or investing in depreciating assets can lead to major financial troubles. Moreover, establishing such spending habits early on makes it much more challenging to break them later on.

It isn't simply a matter of learning to manage your expenses better. Nor should it be something you put off dealing with later in life. As you progress financially, your expenses will also grow exponentially.

You might spend indiscriminately now, expecting to be able to start saving in your 30s and 40s, but your spending habits will have become a way of life by then. Your additional expenses mean you will be very unlikely to save much later in life.

Financial advisors warn against such debt, citing its consequences: "Bad debt isn't just owing someone money. We have seen it consume clients financially, emotionally, physically, and mentally. I have had clients come in struggling with health issues because of the stress caused by their debt. Some even go into debt denial."

Bad Debts and Increased Liability

Bad spending habits essentially mean you are not keeping track of your money. It likely also means you are unsure where most of your money goes, and you often struggle waiting for the next paycheck at the end of the month.

Extravagant spending that exceeds your income can very quickly lead to debt. This includes substantial impulse purchases that occur more often than not and relying heavily on your credit card to fund them. Individuals with a casual attitude towards loans and debt can often find themselves falling deeper in without making much effort to climb out.

This goes along with ignoring your financial obligations. Either you're using payment methods that drive you deeper into debt to make essential payments, or you're leaving off the payments until the last minute. The lack of balance between debts and savings will drive a deeper wedge in your financial independence.

I have seen credit card debt as one of Americans' most common examples of bad debt. With lousy spending habits and financial irresponsibility, most people start relying on their credit cards to make ends meet, get to the end of the month, or even just keep the lights on.

Bad debt is exceedingly debilitating in more than one way. It gives you zero benefit, makes financial planning much harder, and continuously levies a considerable cost on your income. Your financial options can become seriously limited as your liability increases.

Common Bad Money Habits

Fortunately, identifying and curbing spending habits that lead to bad debt is a simple and effective solution:

Ignoring your credit report

One of the financial habits that people in their 20s first fall victim to is not keeping track of their income and spending. More specifically, going further into debt without keeping track of what you owe. Your credit report is a statement of information about your credit history and current situation, which includes your credit accounts, payment history, and creditors' names.

Many people often neglect to check their credit reports for a variety of reasons. Young people especially might avoid this, constantly fearing what they will find in it. However, despite how good or bad your credit is, neglecting to check it can cause many issues.

For example, an estimated 20% of all credit reports have been found to have some error, showing a lower score than expected. That translates to only qualifying for higher interest rates for future loans.

More importantly, being in touch with your finances gives you the power to work towards improving them. It can also give you a better sense of where your financial planning is going wrong and the changes you need to make.

Your credit isn't just essential to secure future loans; it can also impact other areas of your life. For example, potential employers and landlords may also check your report, based on which they may make their decisions regarding your application.

Buying expensive wine with dinner

We all like to splurge every now and then. When special occasions call for celebration, I should be able to indulge myself. However, making splurging a habit is a frequently seen financial decision that can cause a lot of economic damage.

Making it a habit to buy expensive wine with dinner is a financial blunder for many reasons. For one, it is not an essential expense, nor does it reflect a worthwhile investment. When your goal is to be financially responsible, buying things you don't need hinders its achievement.

Moreover, unless you are a wine connoisseur, it is unlikely you can tell much of the difference between expensive and cheap wines. It is a known fact that restaurants especially tend to mark up their wines, but it is also true that price is not a necessary guarantee of quality.

It is more viable to save up the money you would otherwise have spent on expensive drinks. This should also give you a chance to try out other affordable options, and you might even enjoy them!

Having an app addiction

Being obsessed with any object or activity beyond the point of health interest can be dangerous. In a world of smartphones and easy internet access, app addictions are becoming common, especially among young people. This is especially true since the pandemic when much of our interactions and social engagement moved online.

Having an app addiction can play havoc on your finances. It will drive you to spend every available cent on purchasing the game and supplementing ridiculous in-app purchases with no real-life value. Soon, that ceases to be enough, and you start spending money you don't even have.

Additionally, you spend all your time on an app, be it social media or gaming, instead of finding a constructive and productive use of your time. This way not only are you wasting money that could be better spent or saved, you are actively engaged in an activity where you are in no position to earn back that money.

A car can sometimes be a risky investment, considering it is a depreciating asset. While necessary, it should be following your financial situation and future plans. If you are looking to make a long-term investment in a car that you plan on using for years to come, leasing is a poor financial choice.

It makes sense for someone who plans to and can get a new car every three years, but not for a longer-term purchase. The higher upfront costs that come with the lease also challenge your finances.
On the other hand, buying a car will help you build up equity in an asset you own. A lease also comes with mileage limits, which are impractical for anyone whose work takes them beyond those limits. Overall, a lease will cost you more than outright buying a car.

Overdrawing on your account may seem like a viable option in the case of need. It can be when you pay off that amount immediately, which is rare. Overdraft protection, for example, is an excellent way to cap your spending, so you don't go too far into debt. However, even these may incur charges or interest.

Additionally, if you link your checking account, funds are transferred automatically to cover the overdraft difference.

Making it a habit means you might often be spending money without realizing it, leading you to a precarious financial position.

Overdrafting will most likely result in fees. You must pay these until you deposit the money to cover the overdrawn difference. In addition to costing you heavily, If you stay overdrawn, you could lose your account altogether.

Having a gym membership even when you don't go to the gym

This is a simple question of the investment-to-returns ratio. Going to the gym for a regular workout is a healthy practice. It keeps you in shape and active and can also be a great way to socialize with like-minded individuals. However, it's no secret that gym memberships can be expensive.

The equipment and trainers, along with rental fees and special services, make it an expensive hobby to keep. It works out well if you plan for the expense, but it can be highly redundant if you never use the monthly services you pay for.

Not only does it create an unnecessary expense, but you're also not seeing any returns on it. With time, the money you will have spent on services you never used will become a significant amount that could have been invested elsewhere.

Adding delays in getting health insurance

Getting insurance early on reflects your anticipation of potential risks and emergencies. While it is impossible to be prepared 100% for such situations, insurance is still a step toward responsible financial planning.

Delaying insurance means your financial planning is always uncertain and risky. Insurance aims to cover that risk and offer some certainty in emergencies. You will likely struggle to maintain a sound financial plan in its absence.

Similarly, the money you saved for other goals will be gone in a blink should an emergency occur. Without insurance, you have no additional financial cushion than your personal savings. It also can potentially drive you into debt if you cannot supply the necessary finances for the emergency yourself.

Being an impulsive buyer

Impulse buying may not always be a bad thing. Occasionally indulging yourself in a cause for celebration might be okay if you stick within your spending budget. However, making it a habit can have devastating financial consequences.

Constantly making impulse buys will prevent you from achieving your financial goals regardless of how much you're making. Any goals you have set for yourself - saving up, buying a car, getting insurance - will be delayed if you overeat your income and have nothing left to set aside for these goals.

The lack of planning with whimsical purchases can also reflect poorly on maintaining the discipline to achieve your goals. Habitualizing it would certainly affect your ability to manage finances in other areas of life as well.

Even more concerning is that such purchases tend to be financed with credit cards. If they happen too often, you will likely build debt on your card with few options to pay it off. Buying something because there is a "good deal" on it might seem like an intelligent decision at the moment, but it will impact your future negatively.

Paying yourself last

There are always bills to be paid and groceries to be bought. You cannot forgo essentials; however, many people struggle to have anything left over after paying all their outstanding monthly dues.

The concept of paying yourself first is one that I highly recommend as your first step to financial planning. It is a simple and effective way to ensure you always have a financial cushion, no matter how tough things get. Set aside a little bit of your monthly paycheck in a savings or retirement account. This ensures you will have something left over after paying your bills.

This is an especially important step if you are planning on making non-essential purchases. Rather than indulging in those first and wiping out your account, save up first. Ultimately, whatever is left over can be used for those purchases without leaving you vulnerable.

As with other purchases, if done occasionally and with reason, you should be able to treat yourself. However, making it a daily habit becomes costly and financially irresponsible. Financial expert Kevin O'Leary shares his thoughts on splurging on coffee every day:

"It costs 18 cents to make coffee at home. So, do I pay $2.50 for coffee every day? No, I don't do that. That is such a waste of money for something that barely costs 20 cents. If I don't buy it, the money will be invested, and I make money every year while I'm sleeping."

Too much money is thrown at unnecessary expenses every day. Even $2.50 may not seem like a big deal for one day, but these expenses add up over the year. At the end of the year, you will have spent close to $1000 just on coffee! Money management requires intelligent decisions and cutting out unnecessary expenses is one of them.

Invisible expenses, such as repair and maintenance bills or impulse buying, are those that fly by us every month. When we budget, we do so with a rough estimate of what everything costs, so our expenses stay in the ballpark. Hidden expenses are never configured into the budget, and they can have already blown out proportion by the time you realize it.

One of the best ways to avoid such expenses is to ensure everything you buy has some utility. If it's going to be used over time, make sure it's something you will use fully. If it is a one-time purchase, ensure you need it; it won't simply be gathering dust later.

It is also best to double-check every purchase you make and the expense you incur. A good idea is to schedule your luxury spending more carefully. This would avoid unnecessary costs and let you enjoy your downtime without worrying that you may have overspent.

Increasing living standards

Everyone has the right to a good quality of life, but it also requires thoughtful and purposeful decisions. Increasing living standards in ways incompatible with your income is likely to have the opposite effect on your life. Buying brand names, regularly indulging and upgrading your car every few years might seem attractive, but it's ill-afforded.

Living within your means is the best financial advice that can be given or followed. Living in unsustainable ways that do nothing to improve your life significantly will also have unintended consequences. Not only will you hurt your financial situation, but you will also likely suffer psychological and social impacts.

Going on happy hours frequently

Happy hours are a relaxing time off after a week of work. They can quickly become a financial burden if they become a habit.

You will incur additional expenses at the end of the week that could likely set you back financially. While the drinks are reduced in price, you are also drinking more, which makes little difference to your drinks expense.

Additionally, happy hours can seriously cloud your judgment, so you spend much more than you intended. So, in the end, it really wouldn't matter if you had already included happy hour expenses in your budget. You won't be able to make responsible decisions at the moment.

Re-evaluating Financial Habits for Improvement

While financial planning involves setting goals for yourself and creating action-led strategies, that's not all there is to it. It also involves reevaluating your existing habits. Assess them in terms of how they affect your financial goals. If your daily living hinders goal achievement, it's time to make some serious changes.

Chapter 3

Good Money Habits You Need to Take Up

With financial goal setting, we establish that your financial decisions are never made in isolation. You can expect any decisions you make - investments or debts - to affect your financial future. The decisions you make in your 20s will determine your economic trajectory in your 30s and beyond.

That makes it essential that you make smart decisions right now which can serve you in the future. The first things I learned during my work was that good saving and spending habits and learning to budget are just some things you should make part of your financial routine. Making sound, reliable investments in your 20s enables you to reap their compounded rewards in later life.

Many people find it difficult to set and stick to such financial goals in their 20s. For some, it is a question of just moving into full-time work, where they want to enjoy their financial freedom and indulge. For others, this is simply something they do not consider necessary enough to focus on so early. People want to enjoy their time and leave the "serious" financial stuff until they are older and more mature.

The trouble with that is that you don't always have the luxury of waiting until you're older. I have discussed in earlier chapters the consequences of financial irresponsibility in your younger years. It can drive you into holes that can be hard to get out of. It also sets a spending pattern incompatible with your budget and income, creating greater potential for negative financial consequences.

Being responsible does not take a lot of effort once you get started. Many people struggle with the bad habits they realize could lead to difficulties, as they can find it hard to give up after a point. However, it becomes much easier once you start working on these habits and realize the positive difference they make, not just for your finances but also for your health and well-being.

It is essential to start improving your financial behavior early on. The first step is to map up a plan, set goals, and begin budgeting. Explore investment options and make a habit of staying updated on your finances. Check your credit report and balance your accounts to know where you stand.

Early savings also work in your favor with compound interest. Imagine if you start saving even just a tiny amount in your 20s, by your 40s, your savings would have increased. With added compound interest, you are looking at a reliable investment. Here are a few more money-saving habits I can recommend from my experience and research.

Good Habits to Good Debt

This may sound counterintuitive, given what I said about managing money to avoid debt. But it is simply a fact that many people cannot afford big-ticket items without some kind of loan. College tuition and buying a home or a car may be challenging without financial assistance. In that case, there is a way to manage your debt to work in your favor.

Good debt allows you to acquire something that adds value to your life. This is debt that enhances your potential to earn and your net worth. It may also include anything that improves the quality of life for you or your family. This debt is good because of how you utilize it and how it improves your life.

A young lawyer from Oregon shares how she learned the value of good debt:

"Growing up, money was always tight. My family had so many debts piling up that meeting even essential requirements would sometimes be difficult. So, when it came time to go to college, I was determined to change all that. I was a bit scared of taking out all those student loans because that was a big amount, and I wasn't sure if I would ever be able to pay it back. Fast forward to today, when I'm a successful lawyer, my debt is half gone, and finances are strong because my investment in myself paid off."

How do good habits lead to good debt? This debt is also measured by how well you can pay it off. Good financial habits allow you to plan your expenses around your debts without adding an overdue burden on yourself or others.

Paying off your debts in time and in a responsible fashion builds up your credit score. That, in turn, qualifies you for lower premiums and interests with higher value insurance and loans.

Good Money Habits

Here are some of the habits that can help you keep your debt good and aid your path to financial independence:

Building a good credit score

A good credit score is a victory in the financial world. It can make many things much easier for you in the future. You can build up credit scores by starting early and starting small. The time period of your active credit history is significant, so use it to your advantage. You should also only borrow as much as you can afford to return.

Opening a credit card is also a good idea, but you should use it responsibly. Make sure to stay within your budget and means and make prompt payments. Stay on top of your bills, and don't let any outstanding debt get too delayed in payment.

If you have bad credit, you can also work on rebuilding it. The first step would be to try and meet all your dues. Figure out a payment plan with your creditors if that works better. It would also be a good idea to start planning for future expenses, so you don't land in more debt.

Staying informed on your net worth helps you remain financially prepared. This will also help you make financial decisions like budgeting and your monthly spending and savings. You must know your financial standing to make any sort of planning effective.

Your net worth is determined by your assets minus your liabilities. It is what you own that is entirely yours. Why this knowledge is essential is so you can keep track of where you are spending your money. It should help you avoid bad debt by not indulging in unnecessary purchases.

High net worth is a good sign for any individual; the best way to achieve it is to reduce your liabilities. This should be an added motivation to work towards resolving all your outstanding debts and avoiding new ones.

Reviewing and cutting back on regular expenses

Some regular expenses we take for granted could make financial independence harder. There might be potential for cutting back on such costs. These can include unnecessary or frequent indulgences that do not make sense given your financial situation.

When you are in debt, splurging constantly is no longer a treat, it is a bad spending habit. If you can afford to spend less without compromising your quality of life, you should do so.

Ask yourself if you really need to be eating out or getting takeout every day. Would it be more economical to cook at home? You can manage your expenses better if you plan out even these mundane, everyday costs.

Eating out most days is attractive and more accessible, but it is not worth the cost when you have to scrape by the last few days of the month waiting for the next paycheck. Instead, plan your meal spending. You would also benefit from eating healthily when you cook at home.

Fitness

While fitness is important, this is also an expense that you should review. If you are overspending, it is a fact that you can afford to cut back on. For example, if you have a gym membership that you rarely or never use, you have already overspent.

If your gym use cannot justify the fees you pay, you can look into other fitness avenues. There are plenty of ways you can stay fit without gyms, such as going for a run. Proper planning could also make a better long-term investment in your own equipment.

Mobile

As discussed, people are now addicted to various social media and gaming apps. However, none of these addictions are worth the financial hole they can put you in. Spending hundreds of dollars a month on in-app purchases alone can put you in a bind.

There is also an increasing push for people to own the latest smartphone in the market, regardless of whether they actually need it. Learn to prioritize and understand the value of what you already have. Buying a new phone every couple of years is financially irresponsible.

Coffee

We have already discussed coffee as a significant source of unnecessary expenses among young people. Spending over $10 a day on coffee makes for bad financial planning. Over time, these expenses begin to pile up.

Plan for your coffee needs according to your financial situation. Whenever possible, make your coffee at home or the office. You might even consider reducing your coffee consumption as a financially responsible and healthier option.

Wine

Exploring cheaper wine options is always possible, and you might often be pleasantly surprised. Expensive wine with every dinner does not make much financial sense, especially if it's not something you can really afford to do.

Review your expenses and ensure things like wine are not taking up too much space. If you do not wish to compromise, include this expense in your budgeting responsibly to avoid later surprises.

Starting a savings plan

Figure out your goal with the savings plan. Determine if you are saving for an emergency fund or a specific reason, such as a training class or a car. Follow the SMART goal principles to establish a focused plan with outlined short-term, medium-term, and long-term objectives.

You also need to give ample thought to what your goals require and how to get there. This includes how much money you would need to save up total, and how much this would involve saving every week or month.

Figure out how you can supplement your plan. This may involve cutting down expenses, especially if you hope to reach your goal soon. You may also want to explore other income streams to help you reach your destination faster. Explore all your options, and always consider future goals when planning.

Allocating ample time to plan your finances

I have discussed in detail why financial planning needs to start in your 20s. The truth is, given the unpredictability of your future situation and finances, you need to start as early as possible. Aside from this being necessary for your overall financial plan, you should also plan early for smaller goals.

Do not wait until the last minute to check any anticipated expenses and figure out how to pay for them. This increases the likelihood of you going into debt to meet a cost you weren't ready for. Start planning for a considerable upcoming expense, such as a medical procedure, a large purchase or a vacation, as soon as you anticipate it. Most likely, you will need to save up for it as well.

Starting immediately gives you plenty of time to make room for the new cost within your existing budget. It also gives you a better understanding of what your accounts would look like after the expense and what you might need to do to bounce back from that. If necessary, allocate specific weekly time to go over your finances and ensure everything is staying within budget.

Buying the necessities

A simple look at your purchases will give you a good idea of your spending habits. Using large amounts of money on things you don't need leads to money mismanagement. If those things are being rarely used, or not at all, your money is being wasted.

Budgeting is the most critical factor in managing your spending. Once you know you're about to go over budget, which could make meeting other expenses difficult, you can better understand when to stop spending.

Your budgeting plans should also be specifically allocated, especially if you believe you might not be able to spend responsibly otherwise. Make a list of your monthly necessities and stick to them. If there's room for additional purchases, go right ahead. But your priority should always be to make your necessary purchases first.

Learning from your financial mistakes

You're likely not always prepared to make significant financial decisions when starting out. We have all made poor financial decisions. However, we should not wallow but learn from them after they happen.

Understand where you went wrong. Make a list of things you could have better managed to avoid such a thing happening again. Review your goals and make necessary changes to incorporate steps to deal with the effects of the mistake.

Work past the embarrassment of the mistake and talk with others about it. Be it a friend or a financial advisor, discuss the error and ways to avoid it in the future. Adopt a frugal lifestyle to help you through the tough times and stick to it.

Making a budget from your income streams

Budgeting is a no-brainer – it is an absolute necessity to achieve any of your financial goals. However, *how* you budget is just as important as the plan itself. It should not reflect unrealistic goals you know you will be unable to achieve.

Keep a clear understanding of all your income streams and where and how it is best to spend them. Do not overestimate how much you have available, and do not budget from the income you do not have.

Stick to what you know you can spend and spend accordingly. Anticipating and spending income you are unsure of will lead to a financial blunder. Give precedence to your necessary expenses, make room for savings, and then consider other possible costs.

Cutting down living expenses

Frugal living comes with financial responsibility. It may feel hard to do so initially, but it has major rewards to reap. Start by making a list of your most common expenses which put the most significant dent in your account.

Sort these into categories of necessity and luxury. Simply ask yourself if a particular expense is something you can manage without, and if the answer is yes, it is a luxury. It may be difficult to cut these out completely all of a sudden, especially if you have been relying on them for a while.

You can start by reducing the amount you spend on luxuries each month. The goal should remain, however, to completely cut these expenses out of your life. Instead, you should focus more on healthy investments you can make with what you save.

Making investments to earn passive income

There are many ways to supplement your primary income. The obvious benefit is they will offer a financial safeguard in case your primary income is disturbed. Your passive income does not have to be too much. You should simply invest to ensure some revenue stream is always available to you.

One of your best options in this regard is real estate investment. It can offer substantially reliable long-term returns. You can also look into peer-to-peer (P2P) lending or crowdfunding, which provides considerable returns with minimal effort.

Other options you can explore include investing in the stock market. While that requires some knowledge of the market, it can end up being a worthwhile investment. Explore your options and get expert advice where possible. You shouldn't entirely rely on your passive income, but it can be a reliable safeguard against future emergencies.

Living within your means

This is about the best financial advice you will ever receive. Most people find themselves in a financial rut because they cannot follow this simple principle. Your spending should not just be limited to weekdays where you live frugally, and everything you save is spent on the weekend.
You need to adopt a consistent financially conscious lifestyle.

Don't spend money you don't have. Going into debt for something that does not benefit you in any way is simply not worth it. Instead, manage your finances responsibly. Realize what your financial limits are and live within those. Learn to say no to friends or coworkers when they suggest activities beyond your financial ability. There is no shame in living as you are!

Being Responsible and Establishing Good Habits

Financial security and independence aren't just about avoiding bad habits. Taking up good money habits is also a significant part of the deal. You are the one who best understands your finances, needs, wants, and priorities, so you are the best person to decide what good habits you need to take up. Just make sure to stick to them and make them a major part of your financial planning.

Chapter 4

Creating a Budget Using the 50-30-20 Model

Budgeting should never be treated as a voluntary option; instead, it is necessary for a financially fulfilled life. You can never truly achieve financial security without a clear and concise budget. Even if you feel you are on a stable and sufficient income, budgeting is still a great option. It has little to do with your income and more to do with planning your financial future.

Your budget does not need to be overly complex to be effective. To anyone who avoids budgeting because they believe it requires too much calculation or effort on your part, I can assure you that is not the case. I have helped many customers get started with their financial planning over the years.

The first step is always to draft up a budget, and many are surprised at how easy it is to create a simple yet effective one. The challenge is always to stick to that budget. The simpler your framework is, the easier it will be to remember and follow. All it requires from you is some dedication to follow through. It can be developed in a few easy steps:

- **Calculating monthly income**: Verify your net income to identify the amount you can use for your monthly budget. This only includes consistent sources of income, which you can rely on to be available a couple of months from the day. Do not include anticipated income or potential windfalls in your regular earnings.

- **Track spending**: Go back and check your statements to get a rough idea of your spending patterns. To be more thorough, spend a few months keeping track of your spending habits. This includes your regular expenses, necessities, luxuries, and unexpected spending.

- **Prioritize**: Sort out which expenses need to be met first. This is likely to constitute necessities, such as your house bills, insurance, and any loan payments. This does not mean you completely exclude anything that isn't a necessity. Make room for indulgences in your budget; just don't keep them front and center.

Once you've gone through these steps and figured out what you need to do, you're ready to start drawing up a budgeting plan. As I often advise clients, the thing to remember is that a budget is not fixed; it fluctuates and adapts to your living situation.

Review your budget every month while keeping track of your spending. If you're noticing a lot of inconsistency in your spending, it might be time to revise the budget and resolve to stick to it. If you expect a change in your income and expenditure, update your budget accordingly.

Why Budget?

We have established budgeting is a relatively simple process. With a little active participation from you, it should be pretty easy to follow and keep up with. Some people, however, do not see the utility in budgeting. Especially individuals who do not feel they are in any particular financial bind don't think they need to budget and can manage as they currently are.

This is the worst mistake any individual can make for their financial future. Budgeting is not just for those in a financial hole or those who need to get a handle on their spending. It is simply a valuable and reliable technique to prepare yourself for the future. If nothing else, it will cultivate responsible financial habits that you will use and value for years to come.

Here are just some of the things you can achieve with a simple budget:

Staying focused

Budgets are one of the most effective ways to give your life a direction. Instead of going through life aimlessly and tossing money at every shiny object you see, you are forced to consider your long-term life plans.

The budgeting process has you looking at your life as it currently is and mapping out where you want it to go. This gives you the drive and focus you need to work towards achieving your goals. Focusing on your big dreams also makes it easier to sacrifice the smaller desires over time.

Keeping your spending in check

As we have discussed before, the advent of credit cards has turned this into a severe problem. Before these, people could better track their spending and knew when they had money left over to spend.

With over-reliance on credit cards, people lose track of what they have and what they owe. This leads to crippling debt on the card when you finally check your statements and realize you owe a lot of money to them.

Making a happier future

When you plan ahead, you secure your future. As we know, budgeting is not only meant to help you reach a single, short-term goal. The aim is to create a financial plan that spans your lifetime until your retirement years. That is where budgeting comes in.

I have seen the effect of early budgeting in later life for people. They tend to have more worry-free years, they need to do less and less to reach their financial milestones, and they always have a plan. Budgeting is an actual investment into your future.

Preparing for Emergencies

Budgeting curbs overspending just as it prepares you for the possibilities of unexpected expenses. With a plan in action, you can build an emergency fund to help you in such moments.

Instead of tossing and turning every night worrying about a new expense, you will rest easy knowing you have something to rely on. Budgeting acts as a safeguard against those kinds of occurrences in life.

The 50-30-20 Budgeting Model

This straightforward budgeting framework is a guide to developing a sound and adequate budget. It does not set any hard and fast rules but instead creates a simplistic process through which you can build your financial plan. It divides your budget across three categories: needs, wants, and financial goals.

This rule of thumb allocates your after-tax income to these three categories to create a simple budget based on essential priorities. The allocation is as such:

- **50% to needs:** Needs are all those essentials that are necessary for a basic quality of life. You cannot live without these things, at least not very easily. These can include rent, groceries, and utilities.

- **30% to wants**: Wants are all those small things you desire now and then. These are things without which it is possible to live and which you do not rely on for everyday functioning. These include vacations, eating out, entertainment services, and hobbies

- **20% to financial goals**: Goals are the financial things you strive to achieve. For example: paying off debts, saving for your retirement fund, emergency savings, or any large-scale acquisition that requires long-term planning, such as a house.

The framework allows you to plan for your entire net income. It is an incredibly effective strategy for people in their 20s who are just starting on the budgeting track. Because of its simplistic nature, it is an effective and easy-to-implement technique. The process can be overwhelming for beginners, so this technique makes it easier as it requires little forethought.

The model was proposed by Senator Elizabeth Warren and her daughter Amelia Warren in their book, "All Your Worth: The Ultimate Lifetime Money Plan." It was designed as a budgeting rule of thumb for working-class families. This was to help them get around financial hardships by managing their spending and preparing for unforeseen emergencies.

If you're gearing towards big financial goals, this method sorts out the process much easier. More straightforward techniques allow for much more focus on the actual purpose and less on perfecting the practice.

Because of its minimalistic design, you do not have to indulge in many calculations to make this work. You get three broad categories to consider, with which you can plan your entire budget. It is also generally flexible, allowing you to individualize the format as is best suited to your financial situation and needs.

This budgeting framework is a kick starter to get you to save up and pay off debt with an easy-to-follow technique. I can recommend the 50-30-20 framework to anyone starting out, as I promise this technique does work to help you create a reliable financial plan.

The 50-30-20 model in use

I started out in a middle-income home where both my parents worked. I never gave much thought to financial planning, and I assumed I never needed to, as my parents were great at providing for my sister and me. I always assumed I would work hard like them, and everything would be fine.

After I graduated college, for the first time, I felt like I had a lot to do in life and no time to do it. I began working in a contracted administrative position for a private company. I was living alone for the first time, not at home or in a college dorm, and I wanted to enjoy my freedom. Pretty soon, I spent every other night out with friends, celebrating life. I was buying expensive clothes and other expensive and pointless things I didn't need and never used. This went on for a while before I realized I was literally living paycheck to paycheck. By the last week of every month, I would be living hand-to-mouth until my next paycheck came, and the cycle started all over again.

It was then that I realized I needed to check my finances. I was deep in debt. I was behind on my rent and insurance, owed a considerable amount on my credit cards, and it did not look like I had enough money to afford groceries or, pretty soon, to be able to make rent at all. I was behind on my bills because I had no money to pay them. Meanwhile, my debt continued to pile up.

I went into panic mode. I called up friends, borrowed more, paid off my essential bills, and then sat down to worry. This was my wake-up call. I started looking for ways to make more money to help make ends meet. This was when I came across the 50-30-20 model. I found some freelancing work while working full-time to cover my debts. I also started using this budgeting model to help create a plan for my finances.

I was in a deep and helpless rut when I realized I needed to change. I used this model to revise my life, and I began to think of my goals and what I ultimately wanted to achieve. I prioritized my needs and set aside my desires and indulgences. I focused on payment plans to cover my outstanding debts and started setting aside money for savings. I had nearly faced homelessness and had no cushion to fall back on.

Slowly, I climbed out of the rut. Today, my finances are secure, and I am out of debt and able to live a comfortable and worry-free life. However, I did spend a few years working towards gaining the slightest semblance of stability after nearly ruining myself. While I regret those years and wish I had planned better from the start, they gave me a valuable lesson to learn that I have since continuously implemented in my life.

Create your 50-30-20 Budget

It's best to gain a clear understanding of this budgeting system. While it is pretty simple and straightforward, some beginners can be hesitant about getting started. The way to begin is to start categorizing your financial obligations.

50% needs

Start with everything you consider a necessity. By literal definition, this should be everything you cannot live without. In other words, these are things without which your life would become tough, and you would face a lot of hardships.

Categorize these things, as well as you can, in order of importance. These can include:

- Rent
- Bills
- Insurance costs
- Groceries

Now you must assign 50% of your total after-tax income to these needs. That means all of these combined things are allocated half of that income. For example, if you make $2000 after tax, $1000 of it should be assigned to your essentials.

The next thing would be to divide that 50% among all these needs. Some payments, like rent and insurance, are fixed, and you must pay the same monthly. Others, like groceries and bills, can be lowered by reduced usage and quantities. This helps you decide where you can afford to reduce costs to ensure everything is covered under your budget limit.

30% wants

Sort out your remaining usual expenses as wants. The things you would like to have but do not significantly impact your life adversely if you don't have them. These non-essential expenses are still important for a good quality of life. Therefore, it is best to include them in your budgeting plan so you can enjoy them in a financially responsible way. These can include:

- Shopping
- Dining out
- Gym
- Vacations
- Entertainment
- Non-essential groceries

Now you will allocate 30% of your remaining income to your wants. Continuing with the previous example, $600 of your after-tax $2000 should be allocated to your wants. Dividing them among these things is up to you, as long as you do not go over budget.

20% savings

The remainder of the 20% of your income should be focused on building up savings. We have already covered significant loan repayments under needs, but any additional, smaller debts can be categorized here.

This will come from the remaining $400 you have left out of your income. Focus on building up your savings. This is a much more durable savings plan, as $400 every month being tucked away can be put to great use in long-term goals achievement.

Accurate Calculation, Disciplined Spending

This budgeting technique requires only some basic calculations. Figure out your after-tax income and start from there. Do not make estimates, as accurate figures help you plan better. This includes getting a good picture of your individual costs. Include your spending patterns from the past two months and use these to inform your budget. Unless you need to make drastic changes to your spending, your habits will likely be more or less the same.

Chapter 5

How to Live a Life of Financial Freedom

Once you have achieved financial freedom, many things in life become more manageable. Instead of worrying about future finances, costs and expenses, you can spend more time with your family and loved ones. Life becomes easier, and you get more time and money to fund other dreams you have always had.

People with financial freedom can live life to the fullest. A burden was lifted from my shoulders when I finally achieved that independence after years of struggle and near homelessness. I sleep better, enjoy my work, and can engage in relaxing activities without worrying. My family is well-cared for, and I haven't had to worry about money for a long time.

Taking Advantage of your 20s

Your 20s are often considered the prime of your life. You achieve financial freedom as early as possible because these are the years you will have the most energy and drive towards yourself. The coming years will bring additional responsibilities and roles you will have to take on and play.

At this stage, all you have to think about and consider is yourself. With financial certainty, you have the time, money, and energy to pursue other dreams as you progress through your career. That is not to say you will not be able to enjoy yourself once you've outgrown this age bracket. Different stages of life have other demands, and this stage is the best time to achieve independence as quickly as possible to make full use of it.

The opportunities available to you as a 20-something financially independent person are different, just as the challenges you face at this stage compared to later life. Some of the reasons why your 20s are the prime of your life are:

Energy and motivation

In your 20s, you are just starting out with fresh eyes and perspective on the world. Instead of being set in your habits, you have the opportunity to learn. This is where creating sound and lifelong habits come in. This is not limited to your financial habits but all the good practices you might pick up. These can be little hacks that make everyday life easier or methods that improve the quality of life. Once you are set in your ways in later life, good or bad habits become harder to break.

This phase of emerging adulthood is also when most people report their biggest drive to make their dreams a reality appears. That is not to say that anyone older lacks motivation and interest, but as many people find this their first opportunity to strive towards their goal, they own the challenge. You can start actively engaging in experiences leading to that goal and help you set new habits.

You also have the opportunity to start learning those skills you will be using for the rest of your life. While you feel like a beginner, since you cannot acquire these skills with just college or on the first day of your job, this sets you on the right path.

Your 20s give you the opportunity to explore many different options, which is harder to do when you settle into a career later in life. At this stage, however, you have greater passion and are more willing to take risks. Someone in their 20s has little to lose, so they are often ready to go further.

This substantially increases your earning potential and, therefore, the ability to save. You set out, learn, experiment, and find different avenues of interest for yourself. You then use these to generate revenue streams and discover financially responsible behaviors.

Your 20s are also the time when you develop a new family. You move out of the house into college, where you meet many like-minded individuals to create lifelong bonds. You move into the corporate sphere, out of your usual circle, and meet people from all walks of life. These opportunities give you valuable insight into how the world works and how people live.

It also allows you to develop valuable connections that you can use to progress in life. You grow out of who you used to be and give yourself a chance to become someone you know and to define yourself. Whoever you choose to become will likely stick around for a while, so this is a time for reflection on your true self.

You also have fewer burdens and responsibilities to consider. Most 20-year-olds are not married or have kids. Many are not even in serious relationships. This is your opportunity to make full use of this time for yourself before you move ahead in life. You will get plenty of chances to start a family later on, but right now, you have the opportunity to focus only on yourself.

Moving beyond independence

Once financial independence has been achieved, you have the opportunity to look beyond those initial goals you set yourself. This does not mean you stop adhering to the plan you made up for your financial stability. That should go along with how you plan your next life stage. You now have time and the resources to focus on other dreams and hobbies you may have had.

Again, you should approach your new goals with the same technique as your financial goals. Use the same organizational principles, set new goals, and adjust your budget. The difference now is that you have already achieved independence, and you can now indulge yourself more. This does not mean you become financially irresponsible; instead, you must continue applying the good money habits you have already learned to every sphere of your life.

Looking into the Future

With that said, you should consider how best to invest in your future. Your savings are collecting compounded interest and growing year by year, but you can also turn them into more direct passive income streams. Given everything you will have now learned about money management, you are equipped to use this knowledge and turn it into a rewarding investment.

Many people might wonder why an investment may be necessary at this stage, now that your finances are under good management. The answer is simple; savings just aren't enough. You can build up a sufficient emergency fund to last a few months. Beyond that, your savings can't do much. Investing, however, offers new options.

A Wall Street financial advisor explains:

"I see investing as the next big step in the financial journey. You've got this money, and it's just sitting there, returning a little interest. When you invest, you put that money back to work and build wealth. With smart investment, your money could outpace inflation to rise in value."

Your investments can return earnings in one of two ways. Compounding occurs when earnings or dividends are generated on an investment, which are then reinvested. Further earnings are generated from that reinvestment, and so the cycle continues.

The second way is with the risk and return principle. The risk is the chance of your investment producing a return lower than what you invested in or even what you expected to gain from it. The return is the amount of money you earn over the investment.

Using your savings to make worthwhile investments can potentially and substantially increase the returns you would otherwise receive on them. Certain kinds of investments also come with other benefits, such as dividend benefits that act as a reward to investors.

You can also maintain liquid assets that are always available in case you need cash. You get significantly higher returns on a much lower investment than savings. That allows you to invest small amounts in a more extensive portfolio, thereby spreading the risk.

There are many ways you can get started with investment. Some of your best options include:

Index funds

An index fund tracks the components and returns of a market index. These are used to measure the stock market, or a subset used to assess market performance, by comparing current stock prices with past prices. An index fund will usually be an investment in all the components of the index. You may hire fund managers who ensure the fund performs as the index does.

The first step is to pick the index that you want. You can start with the popular broad index, which tracks several different companies. Otherwise, you can choose a specific industry, style, or country index based on the fast-growing companies they emphasize.

Once you have chosen your index, you must select the right fund option. You should make this choice based on a few factors. The most optimal option is the index fund that:

- Most closely tracks the index performance
- Costs the least amount of money to operate and invest in
- Has fewest associated limitations or restrictions that might curb your investment

Once you've considered all the factors and chosen an index fund, you can look to open a brokerage account to begin investing. You also have the option to open an account directly with the provider. Check what either option will cost you since brokerage may have additional fees. However, many investors like myself prefer to have all our funds in one account.

Mutual funds

Mutual funds pool investments from many different investors in a collective scheme. They can be a simpler starting point for many as you will not have to deal with the entire investment process yourself. As an investor, you would buy shares from the company hosting the fund.

Mutual funds come in a few varieties, including:

- **Money-market funds**: low-risk, high-quality, short-term investments
- **Bond funds:** risk varies depending on the type of bonds
- **Stock funds:** investments in corporate stock, including growth, income, and index funds

- **Target date funds:** long-term investments with a mix of stocks, bonds, and other assets

You can buy fund shares directly from the fund or through a broker. If you decide mutual funds investment isn't for you, you can sell the shares back to the fund anytime. Keep in mind you may be charged additional expense fees by the fund after you invest.

Stocks

The publicly listed stocks on the stock exchange are what most people understand by this type of investment. However, there are many different types of stocks available, each with their own unique characteristics that can make for a suitable investment.

Common and Preferred Stock

These are the ordinary shares that generate dividends from the company's profits. These are only paid out after holders of preferred stock have been paid. The difference between the two types is that preferred stockholders also get paid if the company is dissolved; however, it does not come with any voting rights.

You can always invest in stocks directly. You can go through a broker if you don't feel like you have the skills or understanding to handle the investment. An online brokerage account will let you manage all your assets efficiently. Otherwise, you can always work directly with a professional to manage your portfolio.

Income Stocks

Income stocks are regular income sources that offer dividends on the company's earnings. They are usually higher than the market average and are considered suitable investments. Because of low volatility, these stocks are preferable for those who do not wish to take on too much risk.

Many investors prefer these stocks because they tap into the company's growth profit. Additionally, they provide a steady revenue stream to act as passive income. This is an excellent option if you want to save up and need a consistent income or for older individuals who have already retired.

Green Stocks

It is also possible to support companies you believe in morally through investing. Green stocks are investments associated with companies involved in environmental protection. The clear benefit of such an investment is that you can play your part in reducing pollution in addition to generating returns.

Green stocks are bought and sold just like other company stocks. What you should focus on is business operations to ensure their objective to be clean matches their actions. Your options include anything from renewable energy and waste reduction to pollution control and water investments.

Hedge funds

Like mutual funds, hedge funds pool money from investors to buy investments. The difference is that they use more aggressive investment strategies and are not limited like mutual funds. They can also invest in assets mutual funds cannot touch, such as art, currency, or real estate. Their riskier strategies produce returns even in bearish market conditions.

Hedge funds often require substantial investments to participate. Because of their low risk and ability to always generate returns, they are considered a good investment. On average, they are known to offer returns of over 10%.

Diversifying Portfolio to Maximize Returns

Once you start looking into investments, you will want to explore multiple options. Your investments are what make up your portfolio, and diversification is the key to making a sound investment portfolio. This means you incorporate a variety of assets and investments. The purpose of this is to spread out the risk you have taken over multiple acquisitions, reducing the chances of losing your money.

For anyone looking to invest, this is the best financial advice I or anyone else can give you. Do not put all your eggs in one basket, as you will take a risk-all approach. Look into various options and find a suitable variety. You don't have to worry too much about what a good portfolio looks like. As long as your investments are spread out over assets that aren't directly tied to each other, you will have reduced your risk and increased the chances of returns.

Conclusion

Becoming financially independent in your 20s is the best decision you can make for your present and future self. Making worthwhile investments, saving up, and being economically conscious will take you a long way on the journey. The focus on establishing short-, medium-, and long-term goals will help you achieve this milestone.

Financially independent individuals in their 20s continue to thrive in their later lives. Establishing good financial habits early on takes care of later financial burdens, and better prepares you for the uncertainties of life. It will keep you financially firm and give you the freedom to fulfill your dreams.

Managing Money, Saving, and Investing

Your freedom is achieved with the way you approach and handle your money. Using SMART money management techniques, there is no reason why you shouldn't be able to build up your life and achieve your financial goals. Such practices are about keeping you proactive and focused on how you spend your money.

Focus on worthwhile investments and savings. Even if you are going into a bit of debt for investment, as long as it is geared to produce a return, it is a good debt for your finances. Instead of letting your money gather dust in a savings account, you can use it by making smart investments. Put your money towards different assets that can increase your net worth and improve your financial standing.

Preparing Now, Indulging Later

While it is true this requires you to be a bit of a saver in your 20s, it is completely worth it. While many people prefer to spend this time partying or enjoying their "prime years" by indulging themselves, this is really the time to be responsible. It may feel like you are not getting the most out of life by constantly splurging, but this is a real investment in your future.

Once you have financially established yourself, you will be able to return to all those comforts you think you missed from a stronger position. This time, you will actually be able to enjoy yourself without worrying about whether you can afford to do so or not.

The lure of indulging in your 20s may be strong, but it is nothing like the satisfaction of never having to worry about your financial future again. Making smart decisions now will set you up for the rest of your life. You may not feel like this is the age for you to think about budgeting, but this is the best opportunity you will have to secure your future.

You're not Alone in your Financial Journey

I understand financial responsibility is a big task, and it can be daunting to undertake alone. This is why I, and my team at the Investments Working Group are committed to helping people make the right financial choices to secure their future. My books take input from financial experts and advisors and have helped hundreds achieve their dream of financial independence.

The task may be challenging for individuals just starting their financial planning, but I am here for that. Years of experience in the field have given me and my team of advisors the tools we need to help you on your way to stability. Our goal is to help you make your present and future life successful.

www.ingramcontent.com/pod-product-compliance
Lightning Source LLC
Chambersburg PA
CBHW072119150726
47999CB00005B/2033